"To read this book is to read the heart and soul of Carol Fleming Head. It is an outpouring of her innermost hopes, fears, and convictions. Her deeply held faith in a loving, personal God is evident in every poem and story. Her relationship with Jesus is abundantly clear in her writing. The stories of friends' trials, tribulations, joy and triumphs interspersed among the poems make the book an exceptional work. Carol has an uncanny knack for putting feelings, beliefs and thoughts into words. This volume is a wonderful expression of the adoration of God and love for one's neighbors and friends. In short, this is a great inspirational read."

Dr. Lewis McAfee
Superintendent, Union County Schools, Blairsville, GA

****

"Carol's collection of short stories, poems, and prayers are witty, thought provoking, and inspirational. Her writings will capture the minds of both the young and the young-at-heart. I absolutely loved this book."

Ben B. Lewis, Senior Pastor
First United Methodist Church of Union County

A Sprinkling of Heaven's Dust

Carol Fleming Head

authorHOUSE

AuthorHouse™
1663 Liberty Drive, Suite 200
Bloomington, IN 47403
www.authorhouse.com
Phone: 1-800-839-8640

© 2009 Carol Fleming Head. All rights reserved.

No part of this book may be reproduced, stored in a retrieval system, or transmitted by any means without the written permission of the author.

First published by AuthorHouse 4/29/2009

ISBN: 978-1-4389-5479-0 (sc)

Library of Congress Control Number: 2009901510

Printed in the United States of America
Bloomington, Indiana

This book is printed on acid-free paper.

This book of poems and prose is dedicated to the glory of God and to the people who, over the years, have greatly influenced my life and the lives of those I love. God's love is very real in our family and has sustained us through some very difficult times. He has kept us enveloped in His grace and blessed us in all our endeavors. I owe so much to so many for the love, encouragement and faith they have shown in me.

First and foremost, my husband, Bob. He has supported me in this endeavor with love and encouragement through the years and I would never have attempted it without his faith in me.

Also, our children and grandchildren have requested this printing through the years and I appreciate them so much. Their lives are reflected in several of the poems and it has been a constant blessing watching them grow into fine adults. We are truly blessed.

So many friends have offered encouragement. A special friend, Robin Mull, continued to push me to get started and volunteered to do the typing. Dianne Bauman did the proofreading and suggested corrections where needed. Heather McNutt helped put the final touches in order and prayed with me before we released the finished manuscript to the publisher for printing.

I am so blessed in many ways and I pray God will be able to use this book to His glory and that each person who reads it will find a personal inspiration and healing in its pages.

God Bless,

Carol Fleming Head

"HEAVEN'S DUST"

When things go wrong in the course of a day,
And all that you do seems done the wrong way,
Take just a minute, be quiet, be still.
Reflect on your joys and God will reveal
His blessings for you. Believe, hope and trust,
And He'll sprinkle you gently with **"Heaven's Dust".**

THE RIGHT PATH

The eight year old twins, John and Jim woke up very early because it was a magical day. It was their ninth birthday and they could not be more excited. They suspected each of them would receive a new bicycle and much planning had been going on as to exactly what they would do on this day. They knew they were having a party late in the afternoon and a lot of their friends would be there, but the temptation to take those beautiful new bikes on a long ride was just too great. The boys planned to leave immediately after breakfast. Their food was inhaled in unusually short order. As they started to leave the table their Mom reminded them of the party, the time they needed to begin getting ready and also, she might need some help. Both John and Jim promised to be back in time to take care of everything.

Suddenly, they were off. The bicycles were just perfect! John's was red and Jim's was blue. Just like they had requested. They started down the street and their Mom waved as they turned the corner. The plan was in order. They peddled faster and faster. There was a trail near their house that went up into the mountains and down the other side. Neither boy had been on this trail before and this is what they had chosen to do for their birthday, on their brand new bikes. They did not know how far it was or how long it would take. They also forgot that their Dad had told them how dangerous the trail was and how several people had been injured while biking there. It was just very important to tackle the trail on a special day, especially their birthday.

The boys had been traveling up the trail for a little while when Jim decided he had gone far enough and was ready to turn around and start home. John said, "Oh, no! We must finish like we planned. It really won't count if we don't." Jim said, "Well I want to go home and help Mom, just like we promised. After all, it is a party for us, remember?" "I remember" said John, "but I am going to the end of the trail whether you go or not."

At that point Jim turned around and started home, alone. He worried about leaving John but he worried more about not fulfilling the promise made to his Mom.

John continued to follow the trail to the top of the mountain and suddenly he found himself going down. He was going a lot faster than he was able to peddle. He came to a fork in the trail and he did not know which way to go. Finally, he decided the right one would get him home more quickly. There was no way he could know that this trail led into the deep, dark forest. The other would have carried him home almost as fast as Jim was able to get there. It wasn't long until John discovered he was lost! He had no idea where he was or which way he was to go. He was walking by now, pushing his bike and getting very tired. Suddenly, he knew! He was lost!

It was time for the party to get underway. Everyone was there except John! Jim had arrived at the house in plenty of time to help in the preparation and get dressed for the party, but John had not yet arrived. Because everyone was wondering about John's whereabouts, Jim decided he had to tell where they had been earlier in the day. Needless to say, this caused a panic.

Search teams were formed and everyone headed toward the mountain trail, forgetting all about the birthday party. They searched into the night before John was found, scared, dirty, bruised, scratched, but otherwise in good condition. What upset him the most was the failed birthday party.

It took a few days for everything to get back to normal and for some very frustrated parents to allow one twin in particular to ride his bike. He, in turn, learned a very important lesson. From that day forward, he listened and tried to do what he was told. Neither John nor Jim ever forgot their ninth birthday and those beautiful new bikes.

This story could apply to each of us today. We go to church, hear the word of God, know what we are supposed to do but sometime go in the opposite direction. If we stay in God's will and walk the way He has shown, how much easier life is and how great the rewards. If we choose to walk outside His teachings and desires then we always seem to make trouble, not only for ourselves, but all those who love us.

WHOLE THOUGH BROKEN

It's only when we're broken God can fix us,

For then and only then do we surrender our control!

He takes the broken pieces and He loves them,

And tenderly and once again,

He makes them truly whole!

****

There are times when we as Christians are faced with the trials of life that seem to pull us down in spite of everything we do. We seem burdened with problems, confused with life and cannot decide which way to go. These are the times that friends seem far away and we get the feeling no one understands. This is also the time for us to turn our problems over to the greatest friend we have. JESUS! He wants us to give Him our life and our problems and He assures us that through Him, we can all be made whole.

PRAISE THE LORD

Praise the Lord,
Praise the Lord,
For He is wonderful!

Lift up your voice!
Lift up your voice!
And sing with joy!

For He has loved us with a love so unconditional,
He sacrificed, He gave His Life, for He is Love!

THE HEART OF THE APPLE

Take an apple, cut it in half side to side. Now look in the center of each piece of the apple. You will plainly see the imprint of the bloom that you might have seen on the tree in the spring. Isn't this fascinating? You might say the bloom is the "heart" of the apple. No matter how big or how small, whatever the color, whatever the brand of the apple, the imprint is always there.

****

We might compare ourselves to the apple. No matter who we are, where we are from, what our purpose is in life, Jesus should be the center of all we do. We simply give Him our heart and let Him use us as He sees fit. Our life would have so much more meaning and purpose if we could only let go. Wouldn't it be awesome to know, without a doubt, that our life belonged totally to Jesus? It would not mean we would be free of trials, only that we had the Master to share our burdens. The most rewarding part of all, we would know Jesus as the center of our lives and we might just make a difference in another's heart. Especially one that is hurting!

GOD ALWAYS PROVIDES!

My mom grew up in a family of ten children. As a result she never really enjoyed being alone. Even after she married my Dad they seemed to do whatever it was they were doing, together. Church, shopping, traveling, even fishing and other activities involved both of them. During the day, work separated them for several hours but they spent the majority of their time sharing experiences.

After my Dad passed away Mom was really lonely. She did not like to go anywhere alone so she would call on her sisters or friends to accompany her to various activities. She was always successful in finding a "buddy" to share whatever she wanted to do and go wherever she wanted to go. It was not necessary for her to go alone.

Mom was in the hospital for several weeks before she died and there was a steady stream of family and friends coming by to say "Hello", visit for a few minutes and offer up a prayer before they left. The night she died she was again surrounded by those who loved her and had shared her time.

There was one friend who was special in every way. This lady had a fishing pond on her property and since fishing was Mom's very favorite pastime, she spent many afternoons at this particular place. This is where she taught her grandchildren the love of fishing. The lady who owned the fishing pond was about Mom's age and she had been in fairly good health. However, she became ill a couple of days before Mom's death. As a result of this illness, she died the morning after Mom, about twelve hours later. Everyone thought it ironic that two friends, members of the same church for over sixty years, should "pass away" within twelve hours of each other. The funerals were the same day, one in the morning, one in the afternoon, in the same sanctuary, the same Pastors and some of the same attendees.

Now you might think this is a really strange development. I don't think it is strange at all! When I became a Christian, God promised He would never "leave me or forsake me" and I am sure these two dear friends had heard the same promise. I believe with all my heart that their time had come to go to Glory and God in His infinite wisdom and love knew how my Mom never wanted to go anywhere alone, so He provided for these two friends to enter the Kingdom of Heaven together.

How wonderful it is to be loved so much by our Heavenly Father and even more wonderful to know that He always knows what is best for us – His children!

MAKE CHRIST KNOWN

Robbie and his Mom were going home from church when he noticed all the political flyers on fences, poles and even in some yards. "Why are all the pictures of those people everywhere," Robbie asked? His Mom explained that it was an election year and the candidates posted their picture so people would know who they were. They were hoping this would help people vote for them and they would be elected to the office they had chosen.

Later that afternoon, Robbie's Mom went to his room to see what he was doing. There she found Robbie, scissors in hand, cutting pictures out of his Sunday school book. "What are you doing?" she asked. Robbie looked up and smiled. "I am cutting out these pictures of Jesus. Maybe if we post them around town people will see them and then they will want to know more about Him and His love!"

• •

How much time do we spend in our daily lives trying to get the Word of Jesus out to the people around us? Do we take the time to share Him and His love with others?

The above may be a very simple story, but one that deserves a little thought. What would happen if those of us who are Christians worked as hard at presenting Jesus to the world as the politicians work at presenting themselves?

THOUGHTS

Wonder of wonders
The love that you give!
Ever so precious
Each day that we live.

Wonder of wonders
New grace we receive.
Then comes the miracle.
"Yes, Lord, I believe!"

LITTLE THOUGHTS FOR BUSY TIMES

Troubles are mere stepping stones to use as we go from walking for ourselves to walking for God. The stones may be hard and treacherous but we get more self-assured after each step because we do not ever walk alone!

****

Lord of our love,
Lord of our heart,
Make me a servant,
Make me a part,
Of sweet tomorrows,
Of brighter days,
Walking beside You,
Accepting Your ways!

I lift my hands
So I receive,
Your grace to carry me!

I lift my eyes
That I might see,
Your wondrous beauty - free!

I lift my voice
To sing Your praise,
You're all the world to me.

I lift my heart!
I give it all!

YOUR SPIRIT SETS ME FREE!

Guide me, Lord, that I might be
Worthy of the gifts You give.
Fill me with Your Holy Spirit,
In Your presence let me live,
Full of Grace and full of glory
Always, always all for Thee.
Guide me, Lord this day I ask You.
Make me beautiful for Thee.

****

"Peace be still" the Master ordered
To the sea so fierce and wild.
Then the waters calmed before them.
Men stood in awe, much like a child.

If He calms the angry water,
Causes still upon the sea,
He can take my anxious burdens,
Set my troubled spirit free.

My soul longeth for Thee, O Lord,
Show Yourself to me.
Let me feel Your presence always,
In my time of need.

Guide me and direct my thoughts.
Touch my aching soul.
Enfold me in Your love I pray,
Only then will I be whole.

****

Holy Spirit, take me.
Holy Spirit, fill me.
Holy Spirit, wash me.
I am clean! I am Yours.

TRUSTING DAD

His little girl was his pride and joy and she was all of six months old. He thought she was the most beautiful child he had ever seen. He seldom voiced this opinion to anyone. He just kept the thought to himself. It seemed, even at this early age, she knew when it was time for him to come home in the evening, and she waited. When he came in the door she was "his little girl". They had their own special game and it was a favorite of both father and daughter, even though it made some members of the family very uncomfortable, especially Grandmother! He would set the little girl on the back of a big chair, a recliner. He would hold out his hands and she would laugh and without hesitation, fall into his outstretched arms. He would catch her, give her a "daddy hug" and place her on the chair again. This routine was their time to share and it was very clear they both enjoyed it.

You know, the little girl never seemed afraid or unsure of herself. She just knew that her dad was there and she could fall safely into his arms.

Through the years I have thought of this scenario many times. It reminds me that we are to trust Jesus and He will catch us without fail. It is not necessary for us to ask. We can simply let go and know that He is always there to receive us and to give us His Special Love. I believe this is what is meant when we are told to "have the faith of a child".

DESIGNED BY GOD

It was a beautiful afternoon and all the creatures that lived in the garden were out enjoying the perfect weather. There were lady bugs, June bugs, crickets, several types of ants and also the dreaded wasps, bumble bees and hornets. Quite an assortment of shapes and sizes. Suddenly Miss June Bug cried out, "What in the world is that ugly creature crawling on the ground? That, whatever it is certainly does not belong here in the garden with all of us!" "I should say not!" said Mr. Cricket. "Why, I can't count how many legs it has and it seems broken at every set. Also, it can only crawl on the ground. Why, it can't even fly!"

Miss June Bug decided it was her duty to tell the new arrival that it certainly did not belong in this beautiful garden with all the other creatures. Quickly she flew to the limb of the flower just above the new arrival and said, "I don't know who you are, I don't know where you came from, but I do know that something like you has no place in this garden full of special beauty". The new arrival just looked up at Miss June Bug and after a few moments she said, "Have no fear. Be patient. I am fine. God isn't finished with me yet" and she moved slowly out of sight of the others.

Time went by and before long all the creatures were again having a grand time in the garden. Suddenly, Miss June Bug said, "Oh my! Look at that beautiful new visitor circling that rose over there. Is that not the most gorgeous thing you have ever seen? I must go over and introduce myself and find out where she is from and how long she will be here".

The others watched carefully as Miss June Bug approached the new arrival. "Tell me who are you? Where did you come from? How long will you be with us? I would really like to have someone as beautiful as you for a friend!" With a smile that was truly meant for all who were gathered in the garden, the new arrival said, "Oh, you have seen me before." "Surely I would have remembered someone as lovely as you", replied the admirer. To her total amazement she was told, "I was here earlier and if you remember, I told you then to be patient for God was not finished with me yet. If you think of me as beautiful, then you are discovering God's amazing love and the effect it can have on each one of us. When we are one with Him, we do indeed become beautiful and through His love we can literally shine!"

Those present in the garden gathered "round" and marveled at the shining example of God's wonderful love and grace.

****

God's love is meant for all. He can take our life and use us for His glory. He can truly make us beautiful but we must be able to trust and obey. What a blessing! To be totally transformed by the Heavenly Father!

THE HUMMINGBIRD

It was a Saturday afternoon. I had just arrived home and finished unloading my car when the door bell rang. I opened the door and there stood a man, dressed in painter's clothes and he appeared to be quite upset. As soon as the door opened he quickly asked, "What do you know about birds?" I am afraid I answered him in a manner that was not very friendly. After all, I had never seen him before and certainly did not know why he was asking me about my knowledge of birds. I said, "Well, I know they fly." I knew immediately by the expression on his face I had made a mistake in not taking his question more seriously. He looked so sad and I knew quickly there was a problem. He slowly opened his hands and I saw the object of the conversation. It was the smallest bird I had ever seen and one of my favorite. It was a beautiful hummingbird. My visitor then said, "I was spray painting the house next door and this little bird flew into the house and straight into the sprayer. What can we do?"

After a closer look I saw that the bird was almost completely covered with white paint. The man then asked if I had a bird cage and I assured him that was not a household item on my priority list. We talked for a few minutes and I asked him what kind of paint he was using at the time. He said it was a latex paint and I knew, through my limited knowledge, this was a water base paint and was washable. It just might be possible to clean most of the paint off. I discussed this with the painter and he agreed. He then, very gently, handed me the hummingbird.

I went into the kitchen and standing at the sink, I began to try to wash the bird. I let the warm tap water run over my fingers and then I would gently rub the feathers in an effort to soften the paint and prayed it would run off. It was a slow and tedious process but it slowly began to happen. Then I noticed the bird was trying to drink some of the water. Since we had a hummingbird feeder I had nectar, so I put some in a dropper and the bird began drinking. Finally, all the paint was off with the exception of a drop over one eye and I decided to leave this since I was afraid of severe damage.

Now that the paint was not an issue, the next question was, "What do I do with this bird while it dries?" Suddenly, I remembered that I had a colander in the kitchen and I might be able to use that for a makeshift cage.

After locating the colander, I put grass in the bottom, found a splatter screen to use for a top, then placed the freshly bathed bird in its temporary home. Sometime later I thought I would go check on my patient. Imagine my surprise when I saw it moving around quite well. I removed the splatter screen and the bird jumped to the side of the "cage", sat there for a minute, flew to a limb just above my head and after a little while, flew higher and higher out of sight. I couldn't help but wonder if I would ever see it again. Oh, I hoped so! As sad as I was to lose sight of this beautiful creature, I was so excited that it was flying again and prayed it would be alright.

Later, I would compare this little humming bird to each of us and our relationship with God. When we are at our lowest ebb in life, He, ever so gently, holds us in the palms of His hands, cleanses us from our sins and sets us free. He hopes we will always love Him and that we will always return to Him. Loving us as He does, He gives us the freedom to make the choice.

HOW BIG IS GOD?

My God is so big, He's strong and He's mighty!
There's nothing that He cannot do.

He tenderly leads and gently enfolds me
In grace that will carry me through.

In good times and bad, He's always beside me.
He makes sure I am safe, wherever I go.

I praise Him each day for blessings abundant.
I constantly thank Him for loving me so.

Have you ever taken time to count your blessings? What is the best thing that has ever happened to you? Did you get that special job you had hoped for? Maybe you can remember when as a student you made a perfect score on a test. Are the people in your family well and happy? There are so many things that would go on our "blessings received" list. But just imagine how the love of God touches us and what happens as a result. He tenderly enfolds us in that love and surrounds us with His grace that we might be comforted. Through Him, we can do all things.

The next time you consider your blessings, you might start with the love of the Heavenly Father first and foremost.

THE MASTER'S PLAN

God had our paths cross, I know that for certain
To experience the joys, to help in the hurting.

We've shared ups and downs, had fun in the process
Never knowing the outcome but feeling so blessed.

And then He decided that we two should share,
His infinite love, His ultimate care.

He put us together to share a sweet sorrow,
That shows us for sure, don't count on tomorrow.

We shared loss together as our loved ones He called.
We leaned on each other so we wouldn't fall.

And He said,

"Just know I am here and I'm in control.
I know of your heart, I know of your soul.

You were dutiful and kind, loving and true.
You must know for certain, I'm so proud of you!

You were the reason for smiles every day.
You were the blessing that I sent her way.

Just know in your heart when all else is done,
I am your Father, I am the Son."

IT'S ALL UP TO ME

I have my dreams, for dreams are free.
Dreams belong to everyone
And mine belong to only me.

I can hope, for hope is free.
It gives me strength to continue on.
Hope comes from within me.

I can always give and through my giving
Make this world a better place,
Because I'm living.

I will achieve and through achieving
I give new life to those I love.
I give believing!

GO FORTH AND TEACH

This world is quite a place
And I am only one.
How can I tell them of Your grace,
And of Your only Son?

You tell me to go forth and teach
Your children everywhere,
About Your graciousness, Your love
And how You'll always care!

I'll give myself right here at home,
Won't have to travel far
To share Your love, Your healing love
They'll hear how great You are!

****

God wants us to teach others about Him. He expects us to literally, "Tell it on the mountains." Some are asked to go far distances to share the gospel, while others are given the talent to serve at home.

We Christians have a very big responsibility to get God's message out. Are we doing this in our daily lives? Are we truly being a witness for God?

BLESSINGS THROUGH VERSE

Jesus loves me this I know,
For the Bible tells me so.

God is great, God is good,
And we thank Him for our food.

Now I lay me down to sleep,
I pray the Lord my soul to keep.

Verses learned when a child was I,
Simple verses to get me by.

Through days so happy, days so sad,
Days so good and days so bad.

And through it all…

"Loving, trusting till the end,
Jesus Christ – My Dearest Friend!"

HAVE YOU EVER WONDERED?

Have you ever wondered how things must have been
The day Jesus, God's Son, was crucified?
What would you have done? Would you have watched,
Or run quickly away, preferring to hide?

Could you have listened as the nails were driven
So painfully through His hands and His feet?
Would the crown of thorns placed on His head
Caused you to moan, caused you to weep?

Upon hearing the jeers of all who despised Him
Just what would your own action be?
Would you have remained quiet or prayed aloud
For all gathered 'round there to see?

And when others had gone would you have remained?
Ask yourself, "Would I have been first?"
To have made an attempt to give to Him water
After hearing Him say, "**I thirst!**"

Have you ever questioned the pain He endured
Hanging there on that old dogwood tree?
Yet, He loved us so much He gave up His life,
That dark day in Gethsemane!

GOD IS REAL

How do I know that God is real?
How can I feel His power?
Is He a constant, is He true,
Each day and every hour?

Well let me tell you how it's been
Between myself and God.
He's always been right there for me,
No matter where I've trod!

I've seen Him in a sunset,
Magnificent in hue.
I've seen in the morning,
In tiny drops of dew.

I've felt His presence by my side
When I was feeling low.
He's carried me through my toughest times.
He knew where I should go.

And when the world would knock me down,
Abuse me with its ills,
He has gently picked me up
And called my wounds to heal.

How do I know that God is real?
I doubt Him not a minute.
For He's my Master and My Friend
With Him there is no limit!

A PRAYER FOR EVENING

Thank you Lord for this day!

I saw your glory in a sunrise,
Enjoyed the fragrance of a flower,
The warmth of a summer's rain,
The beauty of the mountains,
The roar of a thunderous sea.

I experienced the closeness of a friend,
The joy of a child's smile,
Steadfast love of my family,
Peace in the land in which we live.

And through it all
                Your gentle, loving grace!

DEAR GOD

Thank you for _____

>leading me when I don't want to be led,
>teaching me when I think I know it all,
>carrying me when I imagine I am in control,
>always listening, though sometime I forget to pray.

And most of all Thank you for _____

>loving me enough to sacrifice your Son that all
>my sins and shortcomings could be forgiven and
>that my heart might be pure and somehow worthy
>of Your precious love!

>Love,

>>Your child

TEACH ME LORD

Teach me, Dear Lord, to trust in you
Through everything I do.
Help me surrender all I have
So I might follow you!

I know I have a purpose
As I walk here everyday.
Help me, Oh Lord, to show Your Love
In all I do and say.

Just wrap me in Your loving grace,
Stay closely by my side.
Be constant as the sun, the moon,
The stars and ocean's tide.

I pray Your love will flow through me
That some heart might be touched,
And through that touch a soul will learn
To love You, oh, so much!

THE PROMISE

The troubles in life we must face day to day
Turn glorious skies to the darkest of gray;
And give to our hearts an unbearable load
Too heavy to carry and long seems the road.

We struggle, we stumble, we cry and we moan,
Life's journey we travel, we feel all alone.
The burdens keep mounting, so heavy to bear,
We cry, "Won't someone help me?
 Won't someone care?"

*"I care" He says softly, "I feel what you feel.
I know of your pain, I know it is real.
My child let me help you to cope with each day.
Tell me your problems, remember to pray."*

*"Come, I will lead you, look what you'll gain.
Just give Me your heart; Just give Me your pain;
You see, I have suffered! I sacrificed life!
For you to know peace, I shoulder your strife."*

*"Remember when life seems so full of despair,
I'm walking beside you, your burdens to bear;
And if you should stumble or if you should fall,
I'll carry you then, if only you'll call."*

PRAY FOR A MIRACLE

Oh God, I want so much to know
Your healing love divine.
I pray to see a miracle
For this friend of mine.

I just can't understand the test
She's living through each day.
For she has loved You dearly, God
And walked in Your own way.

Can't help but wonder if the faith
Of those of us who care
Is not just what it should be and
The pain we cannot bear.

Is this Your way of showing us
The suffering of a cross?
Does this in any way reflect
Your feelings and Your loss?

Please help us grow each day, Oh God,
And look to You above,
Trusting you with childlike faith
To care for those we love.

A DAILY WALK

TROUBLES are mere stepping stones to use on the path as we go from walking for our self to walking for God. The stones may be hard and treacherous, but we grow more self-assured with each step.

HOPE is that wonderful attribute that provides us with the strength to keep going, even though things seem as bad as can be. It makes us believe that anything is possible.

PRAYER is the key to getting the support we need to make our steps steady in order to reach our goal. We only have to ask God for strength as we make each step and He provides all our needs.

SUCCESS is the ultimate feeling of reaching the end of your walk with a song in your heart and a peace you have never known because you have learned to walk in total confidence, knowing that the Master Himself walks beside you.

CHILDLIKE FAITH

Dear God, You say a little child
Shall lead us everyday,
And yet we wonder how this child
Could ever know the way.

How quickly we forget the fact
That innocence and grace
Can make a heart more beautiful
And give a life a place.

A place in Your bright kingdom
And assurance throughout life,
That your love sustains us all,
Through hardships, joy and strife.

Help us, O'Lord to know each day
New birth, new faith, new love,
And may we trust in that great strength
Of our Father up above!

****

More than once we have heard that we are to have the faith of a little child. We are told that the Kingdom of God belongs to children. Jesus said, **"Suffer the little children to come unto me and forbid them not for of such is the Kingdom of Heaven."** *Just think for a minute about the trusting heart of a child. Wouldn't it be a blessing if we could be surrounded by this trust and this love? We can when we put our trust in God and hold no part of our heart back. Just as children trust a caregiver who loves them.*

GOD'S CARE

God's love, that wondrous love,
Touches me each day.

God's grace, amazing grace,
Enfolds me as I pray.

God's power, His infinite power,
Provides the strength I seek.

God's peace, abiding peace,
Calms me when I'm weak.

A CHEERFUL SOUL

Sometime it seems my world is tumbling,
Seems I'm almost on the ground,
When the grace that comes from Jesus
Takes control and me surrounds.

Then I realize I faltered,
Took my eyes from off the goal.
But, if the Father paints the flowers,
He can surely cheer my soul.

YOUR LIFE

Your life is God's gift to you.
He gives it freely and you live it
Where you choose to trod.

Just remember at the close of the day,
What you've made of your life
Is your gift to God.

His love will see you through.
It will guide you, protect you
Wherever you go.

Don't forget when you kneel down to pray,
Life's blessings are yours
Because God loves you so!

BROKEN PIECES

It's only when we're broken God
can fix us,
For only then will we surrender
our control.
He takes the broken pieces and He
loves them,
And tenderly and once again, He makes
them truly whole.

MOM'S MEMORIES

Moms have a special way of remembering things about their children. The little chubby hands that always picked the flowers much too short for a vase, the chocolate kisses, a bruised knee and a bigger bruised ego, the peaceful look on their faces as they slept, the questions and "I love you, Mom." How wonderful of God to entrust His most valuable possessions to us and how blessed are we because of precious memories.

A MOTHER'S BROKEN HEART

I do not know how I can live happily on earth.
My only son is gone from me! Oh God, I gave him birth!

Why were his days so numbered? Why did he have to go?
I'm crying Lord, I'm empty! You know I loved him so!

He was so thoughtful and so kind, we saw this everyday.
He never gave us grief or pain; He had his own sweet way.

Oh Lord, I do not understand! Why take my lad away?
The joy has gone from life for me. Can't meet another day.

"My precious child, release to me
Your sadness and your sorrow.
I will wrap you in my arms,
I'll help you through tomorrow.

The pain you feel I felt that day
My Son hung from the cross.
I know your heartfelt emptiness,
I feel your painful loss.

Like yours He was my only Son.
He came to heal and save.
Because He died, oh child of mine,
There's Victory o'er the grave.

There will be joy for you again.
Let Me carry you awhile.
Your son and I are always near.
We'll walk with you each mile"!

****

The loss of a child would have to be one of the greatest heartbreaks of all time. Parents are not supposed to bury their children. Even through this saddest of times God is always there with His everlasting love and grace, ready to comfort and to help one find peace in a troubled time. He truly is a big, big God and He can see His children through anything, and always with LOVE!

MEDITATIONS FROM A MOM

I knelt beside the bed tonight
And heard my children pray.
They thanked the Lord for daily bread
And blessings of the day.

God bless our Mom and also Dad,
They lifted us in prayer.
Twas at the closing of the day
A special love we shared.

I'm sure God heard them as they prayed
So simple were the words.
Compared to some great scholars prayers
No sweeter voice is heard.

I tucked the cover 'neath their chin
And then I took my leave.
The tears I shed were blessed ones,
Not those that make me grieve.

I knelt and took my prayers to Him,
I laid them at His feet.
I felt His love had blessed us all,
And that makes life complete.

OUR DAUGHTER

From baby dolls to high heel shoes,
Our daughter takes a leap.
She works so hard at growing up,
Even in her sleep.

I smile as I remember days,
Now vivid in my mind.
My baby dolls were just the same,
My heels a different kind.

A part of me would've kept her small
Forever and a day.
But then I would remember,
That's not the natural way.

For little girls love growing up,
It never makes them sad.
The ones that can't accept it,
Are always Mom and Dad.

A PLAYFUL SON

With a jump and a jump and a bump, bump, bump
Our son comes through the house.
But we'd wonder what was wrong,
If he were quiet like a mouse.

He never walks, he always runs,
And seldom does he whisper.
Seems he's always happiest, when
He aggravates his sister.

His clothes are always quite askew,
With stains and mud and tears.
You can always tell his favorite,
For those he always wears.

You never know what you will find
Tucked in a pocket true.
And if good luck is yours that day,
That something won't scare you.

A pocket full of wonder and
A new, but broken toy,
Are just a few possessions,
Of our precious, much loved, boy.

HOME AND CHILDREN

A boy's toy here, a girl's toy there,
Someone's jacket on a chair.

Fingerprints are on the door,
And muddy footprints on my floor!

I sweep, I clean, I wash, I dust,
I feel all this is quite a must!

I say, I think it would be grand,
If only they would lend a hand.

But the more I clean, the less they do,
And then I get quite in a stew.

Now someday soon it won't be long,
The house so clean, but they'll be gone.

I'll wish by day, I'll wish by night,
That I could see the house a fright!

Full of clutter, full of noise,
Displaced clothes and girls and boys.

'SONJA'

"If we were more like Sonja"

We'd meet each new day with a beautiful smile,
And whatever the task, go that extra mile.

Each friend would be special and we would feel blessed,
Surrounded by those we know are the best!

And if there were hurdles, we'd not turn and run,
But hit them straight on, we'd conquer each one.

At the end of the day when our work was done,
We'd look back and see special friendships and fun.

For you see we'd feel blessed to just be a part,
Of a group that's so special, A group with a heart!

"If we were more like Sonja"!

****

SONJA FREEMAN

Sonja Freeman is a very special lady who works everyday with the kind of loyalty and dedication that delights employers. She puts all the effort she has in each task assigned her and takes pride in all she does. Her smile warms the hearts of fellow employees every day and they feel truly blessed through her friendship.

Sonja was voted by her peers at United Community Bank as Outstanding Employee for the year, 2007. She deserved the honor because of the extra effort she puts into everything she does. Incidentally, Sonja has Downs Syndrome and she is one of God's "Lights unto the world". Thank you, Sonja!

A TRIBUTE TO AVIS

A gentle voice, a healing hand,
Encouragement day by day.
She's always known just what to do,
She's known just what to say.

We've gone to her when we were down
Or just to ask advice.
This has happened more than once,
And even more than twice.

She's always made us feel so loved,
We've felt she really cared!
So many troubles, all our joys,
With her we've always shared.

It wasn't only body's ills,
She'd know just what to do,
But when you had an aching heart,
She'd talk and pray with you.

God gave to her a special way
To demonstrate His love,
And when by chance you talked with her,
You felt Him watching from above.

She's walked among us as our nurse.
Our counselor and neighbor.
Even in her own deep grief
Her caring never wavered.

We'll miss her as she takes her leave.
We wish her well and then,
We'll tell her how she's loved so much!
She is a kind, dear friend!

We've been so blessed, yes all of us
To know this special one.
We ask that God protect her
As we hear Him say "Well done!"

****

This special lady was Union County's Public Health Nurse for years. During that time she cared for the people in the area with a love and a passion that has endeared her to everyone who knows and loves her. There were times when there was no doctor available and Avis was called on to fill in. She retired from that position and now works at Union County Nursing Home where she is still using her love and her talent to make the residents and their families feel special and loved.

A LADY CALLED "MASON"

The following eulogy was given at the memorial service for Louise Mason, a very special lady, a vital part of this church (and Blairsville First Methodist) for many, many years. Those of us who knew her loved her and miss her dearly. We wish everyone could have known "Mason" as we knew and remember her.

Each one of us has our own special memory of Louise Mason. Perhaps you worked with her until her retirement or maybe you were unable to drive and she carried you to the grocery store, the doctor's office or just for a ride to get you out of the house. Maybe you remember her pies and cakes. They were wonderful, especially the sweet potato. I can almost taste them now. Or you could have seen her at church and thought to yourself, "That lady surely has a nice smile." Can you remember getting one of her special hugs on a day that you really felt "unhuggable?" She was the lady who stayed in the nursery of this church for almost thirty-five years. Not just occasionally, but every Sunday. More than once the church offered to pay for her services but her reply was always the same. "This is my talent. This is my tithe. This is something I can do for God and His house that might make a difference." And make a difference she did.

When Louise first started staying in the nursery, Martha Cone's sons, Scott and Todd, were there as were Avis' and Carlton's daughters, Avis Marie and Carla, along with Robert and LuAnn Head, many of the Rogers families, Thea, Lois, Mary Jo, just to name a few. Todd Cone, who was two or three at the time, tried several names on Louise before he finally settled on the name "Mason". It was apparently the right name because she was called simply "Mason" for the next thirty plus years.

Between Sunday school and church Mason always provided a snack for the children. Most of the time it was a simple snack of vanilla wafers and water. No Kool-Aid. It might stain a little girl's dress or a little boy's white shirt and she certainly did not want that.

Occasionally, she liked to sit out in church and she would ask someone to sit in for her. One particular Sunday I was very honored when she asked if I would stay. We only had five or six children and I thought it would be so easy but one of the smallest was most upset and cried constantly. After he had been crying for what I thought was an eternity, the nursery door slowly opened and in walked Mason, her arms open wide, accepting the unhappy child. Needless to say, the crying ceased immediately and Mason and the quiet child gently rocked away the remainder of the service. Afterwards, I discovered she had been sitting in the sanctuary next to the nursery wall to "hear" if she was needed. Children were her special touch, her ministry.

I think of the bible verse, "Suffer the little children to come unto Me and forbid them not for of such is the Kingdom of Heaven". Paint a mental picture in your mind. There you see "Mason", a baby in her arms, leading a host of children down the aisle of the church. She is bringing them from the nursery into the sanctuary to hear Jesus tell the children's story.

God bless and keep you, "Mason".

****

LOUISE MASON

Louise Mason, what a special lady! She gave years of time, love and hugs to the children of First United Methodist Church. "Mason" as she was known by the little ones, sat in the nursery each Sunday and she considered her service as her "tithe" to the church. She was surely dedicated and a fine Christian lady.

MR. C.R.

So many lives felt his guiding hand.
Inquisitive minds heard the lessons he taught.
Whether Bible or English, or history or math,
He gave them the answers, the ones they had sought.

He encouraged success in all that he did,
A perfect example of dedication and strength.
His help was available to all that he met.
Whatever was needed, he'd go to those lengths.

His eyes twinkled merrily, his smile said to all,
"I'll be your teacher, your mentor, your friend,
And when you are grown, your school days are over,
The gift of our friendship certainly won't end."

And so he kept caring as each day he lived,
He kept right on loving and teaching his way.
Those times we would see him, we'd talk for a minute,
And his bit of wisdom could just make our day.

We can't help but wonder as we reflect on his life,
Just how many people were shaped through his touch,
But one thing's for certain, no question can rise,
There's no other man would've given so much.

****

C.R. COLLINS

Mr. Collins served as a teacher, principal, County School Superintendent and was a friend to all students that were in this school system. During that time he touched many lives of students who needed direction in life. He made himself available whenever they needed a sense of direction, or maybe just a word of encouragement or even a smile. In later years he carried his love of teaching into his Sunday School class, sometime teaching people he had worked with at school. "Mr. C.R.", as he was affectionately called, literally gave his life for all, especially his students.

ANGEL IN OUR MIDST

As we walk along life's journey
We meet angels unaware.
Through their grace and dedication
We can learn how much God cares.

Their task is never easy,
Traveling on their earthly way,
And sometime they just grow weary
From the burdens of the day.

We had an angel in our midst,
She taught us of God's love.
Her life was an example,
From the Father up above.

Her road was not so easy.
There were ups and downs and strife.
Yet her spirit never wavered,
When earth's pain consumed her life.

Her smile was always joyful,
You could see God's love for real.
She never wanted us to know,
Just how she'd really feel.

When by chance we'd meet her
And share a thought or two,
Angie left us feeling blessed,
For that's what angels always do.

****

ANGIE AKINS TURNER

This young lady grew up in Blairsville, Georgia, graduated high school here and started a career in banking. She was a wife, a mom, a daughter and a very special lady to all who knew her. When her daughter, Amelia, was two years old, Angie died of complications from breast cancer. She was thirty-two. Throughout her illness she continued to be an inspiration to all who knew and loved her.

TRIBUTE TO MS. DOTTI

It takes a special person to teach children and make a special impression on them. One must be patient and kind, able to discipline with love, have a sense of humor, a heart that can respond to a child's cry (or laughter) and the list goes on and on. When thinking of these qualities Dotti Stephens comes to my mind. Dotti worked in the Union County School System for many years. She began her career in kindergarten, finishing up in the elementary library while doing many "jobs" in between. She was one of the first to arrive at school in the morning and she helped get the morning underway. (She must have made barrels and barrels of coffee during her tenure). A child could always count on Ms. Dotti to take care of them, whether it be a kind word, a smile or a special hug.

You could describe her then, as well as now, as dependable, conscientious, trustworthy, honest, caring, all the words you use when speaking of someone who is truly outstanding. She has always taken her responsibilities very seriously.

Ms. Dotti's love for her family, her loyalty to New Harmony Baptist Church where she served as secretary-treasurer for over twenty years, but above all, her love and everyday witness for the Lord has endeared her to all who know her. She is a very special lady who has touched the hearts of many people.

When I think of Ms. Dotti and her influence on all of us everyday, I am reminded of a song I learned when I was a child:

> "A sunbeam, a sunbeam,
> Jesus wants me for a sunbeam.
> A sunbeam, a sunbeam,
> I'll be a sunbeam for Him"

I sang this song often, knowing there was a special message in there somewhere. I just couldn't find it. I asked our leader to tell me what a sunbeam would do for Jesus and in her gentle way she explained that a sunbeam could guide others to Christ through their special light.

For several years I would remember the song and on occasion I would spend time looking for a "sunbeam". I'm sure I passed many on the way, failing to recognize them as such. But finally, how blessed I am for not only have I met one, she is a dear, dear friend.

"A SUNBEAM"

She's a sunbeam, a moonbeam, she's starlight it's true.
Heaven's dust she has sprinkled on me and on you.

An example of faith and trust in God's word,
When we've gone for a visit, her witness we've heard.

Praise for the Lord is first on her mind.
Very quickly she tells us, "Just love and be kind".

"Why me?" she might ask, doesn't do this a lot,
The Lord's sacrifice changed "Why me?" to "Why not?"

She continues to live for Jesus each day,
And her precious beam has shown many the way.

THANK YOU, MS. DOTTI!!!

****

DOTTIE STEPHENS

A very special lady to so many people, Miss Dottie, as she was affectionately known, worked with kindergarten students in the Union County School system for many years. She was a dedicated, long time member of New Harmony Baptist Church and a very dedicated

Christian. She suffered from brain cancer for some twelve years and during that time she never wavered from her dedication and love for the Lord. Miss Dotti touched the lives of many, young and old alike, with her love for people and especially her constant testimony as a Christian.

CONVERSATIONS WITH "MISS DOTTI"

"Just take two breaths and praise the Lord,"
We've heard Miss Dotti say.
"Just turn your heart toward heaven,
And thank Him for the day.
Don't spend your time in worry,
Or thoughtless, worthless deeds.
Just reach out to your neighbor
And ask him what he needs.
Then as you talk with Jesus
And you pray your daily prayers,
God will know you think of each other,
How you love and how you care."

Yes, Miss Dotti, you're a blessing,
As we come to visit you,
And you wrap our hearts in gladness
With the things you say and do.
How you touch us as you witness.
How you fill our hearts with love,
And we know that God our Father
Gently touches from above.
Through your quiet and gentle spirit
We can feel His presence true,
In the calm and reassurance,
Precious gifts that come from you!

Dedicated
to
Dotti Stephens
in appreciation for
the deep faith in God that
she shares with everyone she meets.

JAMES AGUSTUS BRACKETT, JR.

Perhaps you met him one fine day
A business deal you shared.
You only had to talk awhile
To know he really cared!

You might have been a casual friend
Your paths would cross sometime.
But you could feel this was a man,
Considered to be kind.

And some of us can say he was
A friend, just like a brother!
And if you needed help you knew
You did not call another.

And if by chance you were his kin
You knew him very well,
And you would like to listen to
The stories he would tell!

But if you are the group he called
His children and his wife
Then you will know, without a doubt
You were this man's whole life!

So look around you friends of his
Reflect on what you can.
And just remember he's what's called
"A MEASURE OF A MAN"

Dedicated
to
Junior Brackett
1930 – 1997

JAMES AUGUSTUS BRACKETT, JR.

James Brackett, Jr, better known as "Junior", was a joy to know. He lived life to the fullest, whether riding on his motorcycle, working in his garage or spending time with his family. He was an avid woodsman who loved hunting and camping with his family, a jokester who enjoyed "getting the best" of his friends, one who loved adventure but above all loved his family with a passion first and foremost. He could make you laugh when laughter seemed so far away. During the development of some property in Blairsville, he proved he could literally "move a mountain". He lost his life in 1997 as the result of a motorcycle accident.

"HAPPY BIRTHDAY, DORA"

I cannot boast of things you taught me
When I was in school.
Nor can I say it was from you
I learned "The Golden Rule".

I have not known you all my life,
It's only been awhile;
But you are quite a special friend,
With a special smile.

I'm always glad when just by chance,
We meet and talk and share;
And somehow when the visit's done
I feel you really care.

I look at you and see for me
An example strong and true;
And if I could, I'd like to be
Somehow just like you.

For you are poise and faith and love,
You demonstrate God's grace.
I feel it every time we meet,
I see it in your face.

Thank you for the life you live,
You touch hearts everyday.
Your daily walk continues
To show us all God's way.

Happy Birthday, Dora,
May this one be the best!
You've meant so much to many,
We all feel truly blessed!

*Dedicated to
Dora Allison Spiva*

DORA HUNTER ALLISON SPIVA

"Miss Dora", as she is known to so many people today, graduated from Young Harris College Class of 1927. At this time she is the oldest alumnus and she is still active in her community and her church. "Miss Dora" taught in the school system for over fifty years. Can you imagine how many students she influenced during that time? Wherever she goes, people are inspired by her poise, her charm and her wit. Former students still visit to reminisce and just say "Thank you" to her for the influence she had on their life. What a lady! Oh, by the way, February 10, 2008 she celebrated with family and friends her 103rd birthday.

Jesus asked –

> ***"Do you love me?"***

I said –

> "Yes Lord, I love you so!"

Jesus said –

> ***"You are my messenger!"***

I asked –

> "Where do I go?"

Jesus said –

> ***"Go and help my people!"***

I said –

> "I don't know where to start!"

Jesus said –

> ***"I will guide you! Simply give me your heart!"***

I said –

> "I am Yours, Lord! Send me!"

THE MISUNDERSTOOD LIFE

We cannot know, nor understand,
The forming of a life.
We cannot comprehend the toil,
The loneliness and strife.

One cannot feel another's pain
Or hear them asking why.
There's no way to anticipate
How a broken heart must cry.

We ask ourself, "What can I do
To ease their walk each day?"
And if we listen carefully,
We hear the Master say,

*"Love this soul as I have loved
All of you each day,
And know I've been beside them
Along life's troubled way.*

*I know when I forgave them,
When they gave their heart to me.
They will live with me in glory
For their spirit's been set free."*

THE BEST GIFT!

Jesus gave His life for you and me.

He died that day at dark Gethsemane.

He gave our souls to save.

There's victory o'er the grave,

Since Jesus paid our debt at Calvary.

On occasions such as birthdays, anniversaries, Christmas and other times, we give gifts to those we love. We try very hard to find the perfect gift. Something the recipient will be certain to like. We want it to be very special.

Think about God's greatest gift to us. He gave us His Son! What a sacrifice! What wonderful love!

How much are we willing to sacrifice for God? How much love do we have in our hearts?

MORNING PRAYER

Morning is here, a new day's begun.
Thank you dear Lord for a night of sweet rest.
Please guide me today, through each passing hour.
Be with me so I'll do my best.

Teach me patience, Dear Lord, in all that I do.
On my face let me wear a kind smile.
If someone I meet, be it stranger or friend
Needs to talk, let me listen awhile.

I pray all my efforts will be pleasing to You,
And when this day is over I'll know,
The blessings of life I receive everyday,
Are mine because You love me so!

HOPE FOR A HEAVY HEART

My heart is heavy, Lord you know,
You've carried me for miles;
And I know I must not worry,
Know that I must wear a smile.

For I know Your grace sustains me,
And Your love protects me here.
Help me Lord, I pray for mercy,
For myself and friends so dear.

Let Your truth ring out so clearly,
Let your joy enrich our hearts,
For you are the way so certain,
Let us not from You depart.

FOOTSTEPS WITH DIRECTION

All I saw in the future was darkness,
No more could I travel alone.
I felt I had just been deserted,
No friend could I claim as my own.

All I knew everyday was some trouble,
Didn't know what the answer might be.
My footsteps grew quickly uncertain.
Whatever would happen to me?

Then someone told me about Jesus,
About His forgiveness and love.
I knelt, I prayed and He answered.
My hope now comes from above.

My steps seem to be growing more steady
As Jesus my Friend walks along.
He gives to me great reassurance,
And puts in my heart a new song.

SHARING PRAYER

When Christians care about each other
And take time to let them know,
It brings a special blessing
To a heart that might be low.

Miles and distance do not matter
When we as Christians pray,
For God's healing hand can bridge a gap.
Make life better, everyday.

Prayer changes people. Prayer changes things.
Prayer can change any situation.
The Lord says, "Pray without ceasing."

NEW HEIGHTS

As I walked through day's dark valley
I looked up and breathed a sigh.
For the clouds looked dark and angry
As they blew across the sky.

The mountain top looked far away
And oh, so steep to climb.
I wondered was there strength enough,
In this heart of mine.

By chance I started walking
And then it seemed to me,
A spirit stirred within my soul,
My fears just ceased to be.

Suddenly, I was on top
The valley far below,
Didn't look so dark at all,
The clouds just seemed to glow.

You see I had received a strength,
The Lord was by my side,
And I could feel His love so real,
On that mountain side.

No more will I attempt to climb
A mountain all alone,
For Jesus walks beside me now,
My life, my all – He owns!

GOD'S PERFECT PEACE

There is no greater peace
Than God's perfect peace,
And no greater love
Than His bountiful love.

There is no greater power
Than what he posseses
And sends down to us
From His home up above.

The only requirement,
The one we must fill
Is to give Him our life
And thus do His will.

When we say to Jesus,
"Take my life let it be"
Each day will be brighter,
Just trust Him, you'll see.

---

*God's peace is unlike any other peace in the world.
It is pure and it is perfect and once that peace is felt, a person is never the same for they truly become a child of God. With God's peace comes the ability to accept life without worry for He has said,*

"My peace I leave with you. My peace I give unto you. Not as the world giveth, but as I give."

WE ARE ONLY ONE

We look around us everyday.
We see people everywhere.
We often wonder who they are.
But do we really care?

Someone we see might be afraid
to meet a brand new day.
While others may be so confused
they just can't find their way.

A broken heart behind a smile,
but how is one to know?
And if we did, what would we do
to help a heart that's feeling low?

We see a child who stands alone,
no one to hold his hand.
Have we thought he might be hungry
in this "milk and honey" land?

An old man sits there in the street.
His hands are gnarled, his clothes are torn.
He looks as if he's very weak.
Do we just stare and scorn?

"But I am only one" you say.
"Whatever can I do?"
"I'd like to make a difference;
I'd like to help it's true."

The right choice that we all must make
gives Jesus full control.
In taking this first step you see,
He makes us truly whole.

With Jesus in our heart and soul,
He'll lead us on our way.
He knows how we can help the most,
He'll use us everyday.

We'll be surprised with new found joy
and celebrate God's Love.
Our life will have new meaning,
truly blessed by God above.

Dear Lord, I pray for…

    A sweet spirit in my mind,

    Gentleness in my voice,

    Love in my heart.

So I might…

    Think sweet thoughts,

    Speak gentle words

    and

    Love beyond measure.

NO FEAR OF DEATH

Death is but a journey
From our earthly home below
To that special place called Heaven
And a Lord who loves us so!

He has promised a bright Kingdom
And a place of beauty rare.
He has told us how He loves us,
He has said He'll always care.

We must never fear the Master
Waiting there to welcome us.
We'll simply place our hand in His,
Give Him all our love and trust.

Please Lord,

I pray for:

    Patience,

        Love,

            Kindness,

                Gentleness,

                    And above all,

                        A Loving Heart!

REASSURANCE

The days seem filled with so much pain
    And sometime grief and sorrow.
I find I'm weary from it all,
    What will there be tomorrow?

How can I meet another day?
    There's so much to be done,
And which direction shall I go?
    How can I choose the one?

So many tell me I must trust
    The Lord to gently guide.
That He is always near to me,
    Forever by my side.

In desperation I cry out,
    "Lord help me through this task!"

"I've waited for so long my child,
    I thought you'd never ask."

JUST ASK

When we are lost, if we but ask
He'll help us find the way.
We only have to take the time
To kneel and humbly pray.

He walks beside us, helps us grow
In grace from day to day.
We feel Him there for He has said,
"Lo, I am with you-always".

HE IS PRESENT

My heart is heavy, Lord you know.
You've carried me for miles,
And I know I must not worry,
Know that I must wear a smile.

    For I know Your grace sustains me,
    And Your love protects me here.
    Please help me as I pray O' Lord,
    For the ones I hold so dear.

        Let Your truth ring out so clearly,
        Let Your joy enrich our hearts.
        For you are the way so certain.
        You are present in our hearts.

SACRIFICE

Never can I understand
Your hanging from a tree,
And yet they tell me everyday
You did it all for me.

The crown of thorns, the soldiers blow
And then the pierced feet,
Yet through it all and even death,
Your precious love's complete.

"What makes me worthy, Lord," I ask,
"For just a little while?"
And then You whisper,

"*Precious one,*
You are My heart, My child!"

MY FRIEND

You are my friend and I reach out
My hand to steady you.
You are my sister in Christ's love,
I'll do what I can do.

    I'll love you and I'll pray for you
    And listen when you talk.
    Encouragement I will offer,
    Along your daily walk.

        But the help that God will send you,
        His love, His grace, His care,
        Will heal you in a moment,
        Just go to Him in prayer.

DAILY PRAYERS

If only we could remember
To start each new day,
With praise, meditation and prayer
And in so doing, give the day back to God
So many sweet blessings we'd share.

And if through the day,
We'd pause very briefly,
To thank Him for gifts great and small,
The trouble and strife would not pull us down,
For they wouldn't seem big after all.

So when the sun's rising,
Just pause for a moment.
Release this new day that's begun.
Give it to God, let Him have every minute,
Let prayer be your lifeline, not just your 9-1-1.

GOD'S GIFTS

God's gifts are great to all of us,
        Dwelling here on earth.
We receive them all, along with love,
        On our special day of birth,

To one He gives great courage,
        To another beauty fair,
To someone else vast knowledge
        And a great desire to share.

"Oh God!" I cry, "What is my gift?
        What have you given me?"
"Please let me know and hold it up
        For all the world to see."

No trumpets sound, no cymbals clash,
        Unfilled the days do go.
And still He doesn't make it known,
        I think I'll never know.

Then one night, the house is dark.
        My family's fast asleep.
I think of blessings of the day
        And I begin to weep.

For through His wisdom and His grace,
        He gave it all to me.
My family, friends and His great love,
        Throughout eternity.

God's gifts are the only true and perfect gifts
We will ever receive and He gives them daily.
Our gift to Him is thanksgiving.

THE STRANGER

I went walking in the woods one day
And there I met a man.
He frightened me at first and then,
He reached out and shook my hand.

The clothes he wore were out of style.
He'd worn them for awhile.
His shoes had holes and looked as if
They'd walked for many a mile.

Somehow I was not frightened
Of this stranger in the wood.
His smile seemed, oh, so genuine
And His eyes were kind and good.

I asked Him why He was alone,
Why no one was around.
He said in all His travels
Not a true friend had He found.

I told Him all about our church,
The friends who worship here,
And asked Him if He'd like to come
Since it was very near.

A sad look came across His face
He shook His head and cried,
"My tattered clothes aren't nice enough
For me to come inside".

"I cannot speak in fancy words,
Nor can I sing or play.
Maybe sometime I'll go with you,
But I think not today".

I told Him ours is different
From the ones in other places,
Full of warmth and understanding,
Gentle hearts and friendly faces.

He finally said, "It sounds as though
Yours is the very one,
Where I'd be welcome as I am,
With no one making fun."

My friends He came, He's in our midst
He's here for each of us.
Let's make Him glad He came today!
His name is simply – JESUS.

THE PRAYER WARRIOR

You came into my room that day
A prayer upon your heart.
You were an angel in disguise,
In God's will you shared a part.

You prayed for His sweet healing,
Or a second look at me,
And through it all I knew for sure,
Your prayer was meant to be.

For God in His great wisdom,
Had chosen you to show,
That we must trust and we must love,
And always we must know!

God above is in control,
And all the world He owns!
We shall not fear, we must believe,
The devil's work He won't condone.

For healing is our Father's gift,
We only have to pray,
And we must always know and trust
Life comes in His own way.

He'll love us and enfold us
As we strive to do His will.
He'll send to us bright angels
That will teach us how to yield.

I know He sent you that fine day,
To demonstrate His love!
He's there! He's real! He will provide,
While watching from above!

FAITH

More than once we have heard that we are to have the faith of a little child. We are told that the Kingdom of God belongs to children. Jesus said, **"Suffer the little children to come unto me and forbid them not for of such is the Kingdom of Heaven."** Just think for a minute about the trusting heart of a child. Wouldn't it be a blessing if we could be surrounded by this trust and this love? We can, but we must first put our own trust in God and hold no part of our heart back. Through this total surrender we can learn to trust God not only with our life but also with our heart. Only then can we be truly His.

MY ASSURANCE

My Lord tells me He is with me in the valley.
He's my Guide, He's my comfort
And always and forever,
My dearest, closest Friend!

He'll not forsake me as I travel
And sorrows weigh me down.
His promise reassures me
He'll be with me to the end.

COUNT YOUR BLESSINGS

Have you ever taken time to count your blessings? What is the best thing that has ever happened to you? Did you get that special job you had hoped for? Or can you remember when, as a student, you made a perfect score on a test? Are the people in your family well and happy? There are so many things that would go on our "blessings received" list. Can you imagine how the love of God touches us and what happens to us as a result? He tenderly enfolds us in that love and surrounds us with His grace that we might be comforted and protected. Through Him, we can do all things!

The next time you consider counting your blessings, you might start with the love of the Heavenly Father, first and foremost!

LIFE'S DIFFICULT LESSONS

The little boy lost his battle with leukemia when he was eight years old. Needless to say none of us who knew him could understand why! At his memorial service the Pastor told the children they should not be sad because their friend was in Heaven playing with Jesus and they were having so much fun!

A few days after the service I carried our small children to visit the little boy's Mom. She was still unable to understand why this had happened and was devastated. As we were going home our five year old son asked, "If he is in Heaven playing with Jesus, why is his mom so sad?" His sister answered very quickly, "Well, if I was never going to see you again I would be sad and I would cry". He replied, "There wouldn't be any reason to be sad. I'd be in Heaven playing with him and Jesus". Then he said to me, "Mommy, if I die tomorrow would you put me on some old clothes so I can get dirty?"

PRAYER IS ESSENTIAL

Suppose you are driving down the road and you watch the car in front of you suddenly swerve, go down an embankment and crash into a tree. You stop your vehicle, run down to the car, look inside and see that the driver is moving but seems to be injured. You go back to your vehicle and call 911 on your cell phone. It isn't long before help arrives and you know everything will be alright.

The Bible says to "pray without ceasing". Is this what we do or are we guilty of using prayer as our 911? Do we only call on God in case of an emergency? Should we not do as the Bible instructs us and make prayer a major part of our life every day?

CHILDREN

They're little Lord, can't even walk,
And how I wish they could only talk.
They goo and gurgle, laugh and smile.
Each thing they do makes life worthwhile.

Someday soon, it won't be long.
They'll join with us in a happy song.
So soon will be their time to go
We daily pray Your love we show.

Help us a happy home to be
Full of joy and praise to Thee.
So when they're grown Your love they'll know,
Their eyes will shine, their life will glow!

PERFECT PEACE

There is no greater peace than God's perfect peace!
No greater love than His bountiful love!

There is no greater power than what He possess
And sends down to us from His home up above!

The only requirement, the one we must fill,
Is to give Him our life and thus do His will.

Each day will be brighter, so happy we'll be,
When we say to Jesus, "Take this life I give Thee".

It won't always be easy there'll be sunshine and rain.
But God's perfect peace will always sustain!

MY DAD

You knew he was quite special
When you talked with him a minute.
The smile he wore was genuine
You could see God's love shine in it.

He'd tell you, oh, some funny joke
To make your day much brighter,
Or tell you of the Savior's love
So your burdens would seem lighter.

A multitude of friends he had
He loved them everyone,
But the greatest friend of all he said,
Was Jesus, God's own Son.

His family was a special joy
And he counted them his treasure.
The wisdom and the love they shared.
Was far beyond a measure.

He touched the lives of each of us
In his sweet and gentle way
And the Christian love he spread will live
Forever more, we pray.

A PRAYER FOR ANOTHER

I pray God's healing hand will touch
A person dear to me!
That he will wrap her in His love
And keep her constantly.

I know God hears us as we pray.
I know He answers prayer.
We only have to put ourselves
In our Master's care!

ONLY BELIEVE

I believe in the Father,
I believe in His son!
I believe in His promises
And victories won!

I believe Jesus saved me
For he healed me, He forgave me!
He's my Savior and King!
I believe, I believe!

ANSWERED PRAYER

Thank you, Lord, for answered prayer
For healing those we love,
For saving us through grace divine.
And your gift from Heaven above.

Our doubts and fears were, oh, so great,
Our faith in you not strong.
You sent these trials so we would come
To You, where we belong.

We know You hear us as we pray,
We know You answer prayer.
We should only put ourselves
In our Master's care.

It's in surrender we receive
Your blessings one by one.
The greatest gift You gave we know,
Was your own beloved Son!

HIS PROMISE

I needed direction, a true place in life.
I needed some help through life's greatest strife!

I searched and I searched but I couldn't find
Some kind of assurance or peace for my mind!

Then I fell on my knees and I prayed unto God,
"Show me a pathway that's easy to trod!"

He answered my cry, said *"I'm here to the end*
Forever to be your dearest of Friend!"

Now I know I can ask for strength and receive
His bountiful love if I only believe!

GOD'S DESIGN

'What is a mountain?" some might say.
How did the earth's form get that way?
Was it designed to be like this I wonder,
Or did our Maker this time blunder?

It is no blunder we can assure,
But put on earth that God might lure,
His children from the depths below,
When there seems to be no place to go!

CARING CHRISTIANS

When Christians care about each
And take time to let them know,
It brings a special blessing
To a heart that might be low.

Miles and distance do not matter
When we as Christians pray,
For God's healing hand can bridge a gap
Spreading sunshine all the way.

So "Thank you" for your thoughtfulness,
Your gentleness and love.
For sharing time of fear and hope
Through our Father's grace above.

LET GOD BE YOUR GUIDE

Today many people have hobbies that involve sports such as hiking, rock climbing, canoeing, rafting and other exciting trips. Some of them use what is called a GPS or Global Positioning System. With this device they can lock into a world wide satellite system that will let them know exactly where they are. In case of an emergency when rescue is needed teams can zero in and usually the missing person or persons are safe in short order.

We as Christians have a similar GPS. It is known as God's Protection System. He knows where we are at all times and He protects us as we live every day. It is necessary for us to stay in contact with Him so He can be available all the time, not just in case of an emergency.

Prayer: Dear God, guide us that we might always be in line with You and Your desires for our life. Teach us to trust You without fail.

PRAYER FOR BURDENS

When you're burdened, heavily burdened,
When no one seems to care,
Then take your problems to the Lord,
Just call on Him in prayer.

He can give you strength and comfort
That will aid you all day through.
He may send a Christian friend you know
Who will come and pray with you.

Just go to God for guidance
When you're down as down can be.
It's through praying and through sharing
That our problems cease to be.

HEART'S SONG

This song in my heart is God given.
The smile on my face came through Him.
I gave Him my fears and my sorrows,
Turned away from the pathway so dim!

Now my life everyday is filled
With His blessings and also His love.
He guides me through each waking hour
And watches at night from above.

He's dearer than life and I trust Him
To always be there for me,
Not only today and tomorrow
But through all of eternity!

ABUNDANT GRACE

For years I was told God wouldn't give me
Anymore than He knew I could bear.
And this I believed, no question at all
For I knew of His love and His care.

At one point in my life, my burdens so heavy,
I cried, "Lord don't give me this pain, I can't do it."
He spoke to me then, as I speak to you,
His voice so gentle and kind,

"My own precious child, I give you no pain.
I give you my grace to endure it."

****

God loves us so much and He wants us to know peace and happiness in our lives. His amazing grace is always surrounding us and making us strong. Sometimes our choices may create bad situations and our life goes into turmoil. We must believe that no matter how life may pull us down, God is always there and is always ready to wrap us in His grace and protect us through His love. We only have to ask!

ALWAYS REMEMBER

JESUS

Creates in us

Joy
Excitement
Sincerity
Ultimate Love
Songs of Joy

About the Author

Carol Fleming Head grew up in Hartwell, Georgia, graduated from Hart County High School and attended Young Harris College. The last forty-five years she and her husband, Bob, have made their home in Blairsville, Georgia. They have four children and two grandchildren and a seven year old Yorkie whose name is Brandi.

Carol has been involved in community projects including, first and foremost, the First United Methodist Church of Union County. Through the years she has concentrated on working with the children, presenting children's stories, singing in the choir and being a member of numerous committees. She serves on the local Advisory Board for Adult Education, served several years on the Foundation Board of North Georgia Technical College and has worked in various organizations in the area as a volunteer.

In Loving Memory

"MY SPECIAL FRIEND - ANN"

*She touches everyone she meets
With her Sweetness and her smiles
Whether it was yesterday
Or just a little while*

*She'll always ask, "And how are you?"
You feel she really cares!
She reaches out, she gives a hug,
Her happiness and joy she shares.*

*Life's road has not been easy
For this gentle child of God,
But she has spread His love each day
No matter where she's trod!*

*Those of us who know her well
Have been with her in sorrow,
And we reach out to let her know
We'll be there through the "morrow!"*

*Lord let her feel the heartfelt love,
Our constant, caring prayers!
Just touch her with Your loving grace,
And let her feel how much we care.*

*With love to Ann
Carol Head
January 27, 2009*